CANCER is NOT a DEATH Sentence

An Overcomer's Story

Linda Herron

Acknowledgments

"Great it is to dream the dream, when you stand in youth by a starry stream; but a greater thing it is to fight life through and say at the end, 'The dream is true'!"

Thanks to Pastors John and Dodie Osteen for teaching me the Bible and how to stand, fight, and win!

Thanks to Pastor Joel and Victoria Osteen, Lisa Comes, and Dr. Paul Osteen for continuing to teach God's Word.

Thanks to Jessilee Ford, Lee Andrews, Ginger Kainer, and Tim Parkinson for all their help in editing and formatting this book.

Thank you to the Father, Jesus, and the Holy Spirit for my life and their love!

Unless otherwise indicated, all Scripture quotations in this book are from the New King James Version of the Bible/Thomas Nelson Publishers, Nashville: Thomas Nelson Publishers., Copyright ©1982. Used by permission. All rights reserved.

Table of Contents

Chapter 1
My Background

*W*hy can I be so bold as to say that cancer is not a death sentence? I am a four-time **victor,** so I know firsthand that cancer is not a death sentence. Cancer would like for you to think that there is no victory! But there is! We have victory in Jesus (1 Corinthians 15:57). Cancer has tried to take me out, but *"greater is He that is in me than he that is in the world* (I John 4:4)!"

Did you know that all of us have cancer cells in our bodies? To combat these, we also have cells called Natural Killer cells (NK Cells) that destroy cancer cells. However, when our immune system doesn't work well, the NK cells fail to do their job and cancer cells grow.

A truth that you need to know and have settled is that sickness is not from God. John 10:10 says, *"it is the thief that has come to kill, steal, and to destroy; but Jesus came that we might have life and life more abundantly!"* This verse tells us that there is an ultimate fight for our lives. The Lord wants us to be alive and on fire for Him. The devil, who is the thief, wants us dead and out of his way! **If God be for you, cancer cannot be against you** (Romans 8:31). God is for you! **Cancer can try its best, but its best is not enough!**

You may have heard that *"if it is God's will, He will heal me."* **For your victory over cancer, you will need to get rid of that thought and discover the truth.** This book will help you to know that it is His will to heal you. As you begin to read God's Word, you will find the truth about His will for you. In Exodus 15:26, He says, "***I am the God that healeth thee!***"

Jesus went about healing all that were sick (Matthew 4:23, 9:35; Acts 10:38). The only time He could do no mighty miracles was in His home town **because of their unbelief** (Mark 6:1-6). Hebrews 4:2 tells us that **we must mix faith with the Word** for it to profit us. *"For unto us was the gospel preached, as well as unto them: but the word preached did not profit them, not being mixed with faith in them that heard it (Hebrews 4:2)."*

What is faith? Faith is taking God at His Word and waiting for it to manifest in your life. Faith comes in all sizes. There is little faith and great faith. In Matthew 17:20, *"Jesus said unto them, ... 'If ye have faith as a grain of mustard seed, ye shall say unto this mountain, 'Remove hence to yonder place'; and it shall remove; and nothing shall be impossible unto you.'"* A mustard seed is tiny. So, even if your faith is small, it still will work with the Word if you believe.

Do you know what the Bible says about you and your situation? The late Pastor John Osteen said to "find where it is written" about your situation. The Holy Spirit is your Helper. Ask Him to show you scriptures that apply to what you are faced with, and believe that the Word of God is true. Find the place in the Bible for yourself where it is written about you.

A good place to start is Isaiah 26:3: *"He will keep you in perfect peace if your mind is stayed on Him."*

Focus on the Lord and not on cancer,
and peace will be yours!

Have faith in God, not the devil or disease (sickness). You may not have known where sickness really comes from, but it is a work of the devil.

There is no sickness in Heaven, so it is not from there. James 1:17 says, *"Every good gift and every perfect gift is from above, and cometh down from the Father of lights, with whom is no variableness, neither shadow of turning."*

What is your perception of the problem? I knew that Isaiah 53:4-5 was true. Jesus took our grief and our sorrow (pain), and by His stripes we were healed. I am healed no matter if cold, flu, or cancer tries to take me out. I have the victory through Jesus Christ, my Lord! I knew that this light affliction called cancer was but for a moment and was working a far more and exceeding weight of glory (2 Corinthians 4:17). You can know that, too! You can begin to see "the problem" God's way.

God has great plans for you and for me no matter what the circumstances look like. Philippians 1:6 says that *"He who began a good work in you will* *complete it!"* Psalm 16:11 says *"Thou wilt show me the path of life, and in Thy presence is fullness of joy... pleasures forevermore."*

My confidence and my trust were in my Heavenly Father, His Son Jesus Christ, and the Holy Spirit. They have been my best friends since I was a child. They have never failed me even though I have failed them many times. Their love covers our mistakes (Proverbs 10:12).

You can begin today to have that same confidence and trust. Say this, *"Lord, I put my trust in you and not the problem or report. Please give me wisdom so that I know what I need to do."*

Don't be afraid of the word "cancer" or the doctor's report. Isaiah 41:10 says *"Be not afraid"*. Fear means you lack peace and lack focus on His promise. If you lack peace, you will lack joy, happiness, and laughter which are medicine (Proverbs 17:22). Whose report will you believe (Isaiah 53:1)? Say this, "I believe the report of the Lord"! Faith cometh by hearing the Word of God (Romans 10:17) and knowing God has given victory to others and He can to you too (Romans 2:11).

I made a tape of healing scriptures that I went to sleep listening to every night for over 12 years before cancer came my way. This, and hearing of and seeing miracles of God, helped to build my faith so I could stand.

Nehemiah 8:10 says that *"the joy of the Lord is our strength!"* Proverbs 17:22 says that *"laughter doeth good like a medicine."* Yes, you can have joy when faced with cancer if your joy is in the Lord and His Word! Let the joy of the Lord be your strength! I chose to make it fun and not depressing.

**Don't let your circumstances dictate your joy.
Let your joy dictate your circumstances!**

Several times, I went singing into the operating room (OR). I would make noises like a race car as they wheeled me in. Set your mind for success and progress. 2 Corinthians 10:5 says, "*Casting down imaginations, and every high thing that exalteth itself against the knowledge of God, and bringing into captivity every thought to the obedience of Christ.*" I knew cancer was not above the Name of Jesus. The Lord told me that I win in every situation, so I knew success was mine!

Believe: "Be leaf" - Be a leaf of the tree of life and not death. In John 15:5, Jesus said, "*I am the vine, ye are the branches: He that abideth in me, and I in him, the same bringeth forth much fruit: for without me ye can do nothing.*" I believed I would not die, but live, and declare the works of the Lord *(Psalm 118:17)*.

Deuteronomy 30:19 tells us, "*I have set before you life and death, blessing and cursing: therefore, choose life, that both thou and thy seed may live.*" Isaiah 33:6 says, "*wisdom and knowledge shall be the stability of thy times and strength of salvation: fear of the Lord is his treasure.*"

Perfect peace comes from the presence of God and His love and mercy. He sent Jesus to demonstrate His love. You must know Him. When you know Jesus, His love and peace will cast out all fear (1 John 4:18).

The battle belongs to the Lord. (1 Samuel 17:47) Your battle belongs to the Lord! **Faith has a rest in the Lord!** Be a prisoner of hope (Zechariah 9:12)! Don't let hopelessness take you as a prisoner of war!

Isaiah 33: 2 says *The Lord is "... my salvation in the time of trouble."* I encourage you to *"wait and hope in Him and not grow weary or faint!"* (Isaiah 40:31).

Isaiah 54:10 says, *"...my kindness shall not depart from thee, neither shall the covenant of my peace be removed, saith the Lord that hath mercy on thee."* It goes on to say in verse 17, *"that no weapon (cancer) which is formed against you will prosper."* **Since God is for us, how can disease (cancer) be against us** (Romans 8:31)?

Hebrews 10:35 tells us, *"Cast not away therefore your confidence, which hath great recompense of reward."*

1 John 5:4 and 14 says, *"For whatsoever is born of God overcometh the world: and this is the victory that overcometh the world, even our faith.... And this is the confidence that we have in Him, that, if we ask anything according to His will, He heareth us." "Greater is He that is in you than he that is in the world* (1 John 4:4)." *Believe in the Lord and His Word and you will overcome.* Ask Him for your healing according to His Word and believe Him! *"When you have done all, stand (Ephesians 6:13)!"*

You have victory in Jesus! Believe you are an overcomer in Him! His will is for you to be healed no matter what the report.

Chapter 2

Adventure of 1993

*I*n January of 1993, I felt a pain in my left breast. The Holy Spirit told me to go to the doctor. The Holy Spirit is the third part of the Trinity which is the Father, Jesus, and the Holy Spirit. Jesus promised to leave a Comforter when He ascended to Heaven. The Holy Spirit is the Comforter, a gift to all who believe in Jesus as the Son of God. We are a three-part being - body, soul, and spirit. The Holy Spirit is a spirit and He will speak to our spirit. We just need to listen and do what He tells us.

Jesus called Him the Spirit of Truth. In John 16:13, *Jesus said, "when the Spirit of truth, is come, He will guide you into all truth: for He shall not speak of Himself; but whatsoever He shall hear, that shall He speak: and He will shew you things to come."*

I waited until February and went to the doctor. She told me I had arthritis of the chest and gave me 800 mg of Ibuprofen since she could not feel a lump. I took it for a few days, but it was tearing up my stomach. I knew by the Holy Spirit that was not the answer.

Since my mother had died of breast cancer when I was 13, I felt a mammogram was in order. I did not believe I had cancer, but I thought that was a good step to take. The doctor sent me to a gynecologist who had a mammogram taken. It showed a spot, but they did not think it was anything and told me to come back in 3 months for another mammogram. After the second one, they sent me to a breast doctor who was also a surgeon. The doctor did a needle biopsy, and later did a tricut biopsy.

By now it was June, and school was out. Besides the 1992-93 school year being full, it was a year with many tragedies. A friend died in September. In December, my aunt fell and had successful brain surgery at age 85. In March, a friend's daughter was killed in a car accident. In April, a lady who had been like a mother to me, died. In May, three friends and a student at school died.

The doctor wanted to do surgery immediately. I told him I was taking a three week trip, and we could schedule surgery after I returned. I needed some rest! He got me to agree to shorten my trip to two weeks.

We did the tricut biopsy, and I was off to California. While I was out there, I got the results of the biopsy: there were cancer cells. When I got home, friends wanted me to get a second opinion. I went to see another doctor, and we asked a couple of doctors at church their opinions. All said to do surgery now!

The initial news of my circumstance hit me rather hard, as you can imagine. I had stood against cancer, but I knew this had come to take the word of healing out of my life. I just had to put my confidence in the Lord. I was not fearful because my trust was in the Lord, Who had always taken care of me.

I had to decide whether to do a lumpectomy or a mastectomy. If I did the lumpectomy, I would have to do radiation. If I did a mastectomy and it was small with no lymph involvement, I would not have to do anything. Before making a decision, my sister had me call the radiologist.

After talking to the radiologist, I had no peace about doing radiation, so I opted to do the mastectomy. I had no peace because for some reason the Holy Spirit knew that was not the direction for me to go. Colossians 3:15 says, "*And let the peace of God rule in your hearts, ... and be ye thankful.*" This means to follow peace from the Holy Spirit or lack of it. Peace is a go-ahead, and no peace says "Don't go that route."

We did surgery in July. The night before surgery, I was at church leading worship until 11:30 PM. At that time, I was at a small church helping out.

The next morning at the hospital, the first place I went was the pre-op room where several other women were waiting quietly with fear on them. I was sitting up and humming praise songs. I laid hands on several of them and prayed. That blessed me as much as it did them! What a privilege that God, the Father, wants to use us to touch the lives of others! God wants to use you in the same way when you are walking out your healing wherever you are.

I also prayed with every person that came to tell me they would be in the OR with me. When they wheeled me to the OR, I was singing. One of them said, "Who is singing?" Another said, "It is the patient." After that, I was out until I woke up in recovery and they took me to my room. Surgery went great!

When we got to the room, a nurse came in and said she had heard my friends praying and wanted prayer. I reached over and prayed for her. When people would call, I would answer. They would ask how I was doing, and I told them I was doing great. They were so shocked to hear me.

I am very blessed that as soon as I wake up from surgery, I am awake and ready to go on. I know many people are very sleepy and out of it-but not me. Thank you, Jesus! That is a blessing from Him that I had nothing to do with!

The doctor was so amazed at how well I was doing that he told me I could go home if I wanted. Since I had never done this before, I opted to stay overnight.

The Lord arranged for me to have a private room. According to insurance, I should have had a semi-private room, but none were available. That was a huge blessing to me. Since I am single, having someone else in the room would have bothered me.

We had a great time! The phone was busy and I had a small party. I had about 10 friends in the room at one time. I did have to get help to get out of bed, but since I had just had a mastectomy with removal of lymph nodes and had two drains in me, that was not unusual.

The nurse tried to give me pain medication, but I told her I had no pain. She told me not to wait until it got to be too much. I told her again there was no pain! Read Isaiah 53:4 in the Amplified. It says Jesus took my pain. I never had any pain and did not ever take a pain pill. If I had had pain, I would have taken the medication. Listening to my healing scripture tape for all those years paid off. Thank you, Jesus!

I went home the day after the surgery. One of the nurses wanted to keep me there. She said, "You are too much fun!" I said "Thanks, but I'm ready to go." I was glad I could entertain them, but ...

I went home and had to have a friend spend a week with me since I was unable to get out of bed by myself. There were two plastic drains 9 inches by 3/4 inch in my side. I stayed home for a week. After the drains came out, I drove to church which was not too far away. Thank God, I had a friend with me. I realized it was a little early to drive, but I made it.

After about two weeks, I was back at church leading worship and could raise my arm up and over my head and touch my ear. That was unheard of at the time because of the surgery I had. Usually, women have to work for a long time to raise their arm like that. I had told the Lord I had to have the use of my arm, and I was determined to raise my arm when leading worship. God was faithful! *The same power that raised Jesus from the dead dwells in me and in you (Romans 8:11)."*

The tumor was 1.3 cm, and there was no lymph involvement. Since the tumor was over 1 cm, the oncologist wanted me to do chemo. Being a math teacher, I knew just how small .3 centimeter was. That was not enough in size for me to agree to chemo!

I knew when the tumor started. I knew that it was that size because we wasted time taking Ibuprofen and waiting three months to do a biopsy. My surgeon agreed with my decision against chemo. I tried to eat healthy, and went on with life. Four weeks after surgery, I started the 1993-94 school year.

I had to go in every three months for a check-up. We did a mammogram on March 11,1994, which revealed a cancerous looking spot. I got the news on the 17th when I went in for my regular appointment.

Going into the appointment, I picked up a book to use under the papers I was grading while in the waiting room. The doctor told me the news and that surgery was needed. That meant I had to change doctors since my school district had changed insurance companies. The book I picked up just happened to be my insurance preferred doctors' list. That was the Holy Spirit's doing. We looked in the book and found a fabulous doctor in my new plan.

Chapter 3

Adventure of 1994

I went to the new doctor who recommended a lumpectomy with a follow-up of radiation. This time I had peace about doing radiation. This seemed odd since eight months before, I had no peace about radiation. I had a different doctor and a different hospital, but the radiologists were the same ones. Why did I have no peace and then eight months later have peace? I did not know the answer, but I knew the Holy Spirit leads by peace. The Lord knew why I had peace this time, but not before.

One day as I was sitting quietly, Jesus spoke to me the same thing He spoke to Peter in Luke 22:31, *"The devil has tried to sift you as wheat but I have prayed for you, that your faith fail not."* That was so sweet of Jesus! It really touched my heart and encouraged me!

On March 28, 1994, I underwent surgery. I got there at 7:30 AM and did not go into surgery until 1:30 PM.

In pre-op, my friends and I had a party of praying for others and singing. Orderlies and nurses would come by and join in the singing for awhile. In the OR, I was singing, and then one of them sang a song to me. Then I sang again and went into la-la land.

All went fabulously and, once again, I had no pain! The tumor was .5 cm. This time, I was ready to go home that day, but the doctor did not come to see me until the next day. Fortunately, the Lord gave me a private room, so a friend stayed overnight to keep me from being bored. I went back to teaching 3 weeks after surgery. I was feeling guilty about someone teaching my classes when I was out having fun. I probably should have waited longer but....

On April 27, I started radiation. Before starting treatments, the doctors had to mark the area to be radiated. I had black marks on me that could rub off on my clothes. This was Spring, and light-colored clothing and black marks were not going to go together, since the marks would come off on the light clothing and ruin them.

I prayed, and the Lord led me to a place where I bought three outfits that same day. They were dark cotton knit tops with painted designs on them with matching pants. Each outfit cost only $14.00 a set. I also found some night shirts to sleep in. God is soooooo good!

I was not able to get the marked area wet, so I had to come up with a way to shower. The Holy Spirit showed me how to do that. I got a hand held shower head and a plastic patio table to put in the tub to sit on. It worked great! I had to wash my hair in the kitchen sink. My skin would not keep the marks very well, so they had to re-mark me almost every time. That was really a blessing since after the treatments I no longer had any marks!

I was blessed to have two other math teachers that took my last class for me four days a week. I had treatments every day for five weeks. I would do them in the afternoon, Monday to Thursday. On Friday, I had to go in before school. First period was my conference time, so I could make it downtown and back to school in time to teach. Sometimes on Friday, I was tired by the time I got to school. I did not want to go to the lounge and lie down because my friends would worry. I had carpet in my room, so I laid down on the carpet for a while before class.

There were a total of 25 treatments over five weeks. A friend who had done radiation gave me some of her scriptures to stand on about the Father being a shield. I used those and found Isaiah 43:2, *"when thou walkest through the fire, thou shalt not be burned; neither shall the flame kindle upon thee."* My paraphrase of that scripture: when I am zapped with radiation, I will not be burned nor shall the flame scorch me.

My skin is very fair, so I burn very easily in the sun. Your skin can turn black with radiation treatments. On my 24th treatment, my technicians and I were talking, and I quoted Isaiah 43:2. Since I only had one more treatment, they told be that they thought I would have burned big time. My skin turned a light pink. It did not peel. I just sloughed off a little powder-like dead skin. **I went though the fire and was not burned, nor did the flame scorch me! God's Word is true**!

Since I had to do the treatments, I seized the opportunity to lay hands on all the gowns in the dressing rooms and pray over them. I will only know in Heaven how God used that point of contact to help others.

I finished my treatments after school was out. Two weeks after I finished, I went out West to visit friends and family. That was probably not the smartest thing to do. Every time I go back to the Phoenix airport, I remember how physically weak I was, and am amazed I made it without asking for help. God was gracious to me and helped me to do it. I don't suggest others follow in those footsteps. Rest more than I did!

Rest much and reduce all activities when doing radiation. Take it easy! Don't push! I pushed too much!!!! It was not wise! The Father was soooooo merciful to me!!! You will need to take naps and sleep late. Don't fight the fatigue! Resting and regaining your strength are the most important things! Life will go on if you don't clean house and can't make every event.

A friend told me that the radiation would make me very tired for a year to a year and a half. I said to myself, "Not me!" I just continued on with everything, but did sleep in late on Saturdays and took naps.

Well, when I woke up one Saturday morning, I sat straight up in bed with the realization that I had a level of energy at that moment that I had not had in a long time. My body was saying, "Okay, I have now had time to be fully repaired." I do not remember just how long after my treatments that was, but it was probably close to a year or more.

My spirit man was ready to go immediately after surgery, but my body needed time to repair. After all, it had gone through two surgeries, eight months apart; five weeks of radiation; and a full year of teaching, minus three weeks.

Chapter 4

Adventure of 2004

For about three years, I had to go to my oncologist surgeon for a check-up every three months. After that, I went every six months for two years, and then I graduated to only one visit a year. I got a regular check-up every year. I am a firm believer in yearly check-ups. It gives you a picture of your health and clues you into problems before they are life threatening.

After being cancer free for ten years, **I had another opportunity to believe God for healing.** For several months, a few people had been telling me to stop doing so much for others and take care of myself. Of course, I didn't, so my immune system was down.

I had my annual mammogram in late February of 2004. On March 2, I got the news that my mammogram had a spot and I needed a biopsy. On March 11, I went to my doctor. He wanted to remove the lump and scheduled a day surgery on March 23. Between the doctor's visit and the surgery, a very close friend died, and then the father of two other friends of mine also died. Because of what all my friends were going through, I kept my situation semi-confidential.

The surgery went fine. I had some kind of respiratory, sinus, laryngitis junk that kept me from singing in the operating room as I had done in the past, but I went in joking, laughing, and with a song in my heart. The outcome of the surgery was not what I expected. I did not expect it to be cancer, but it was. The doctor felt that he had gotten all of it, but he wanted the lab to study it for two weeks. He said that we might do chemo. That was not something I wanted to hear!

2 Corinthians 4:17, Romans 8:11, and Isaiah 53:4-5 are true. This light affliction is but for a moment and is working a far more exceeding and eternal weight of glory! The same power that raised Jesus from the dead dwells in us and makes our bodies alive. We are healed by His stripes, and He took our pain. Cancer is a light affliction! His resurrection power will quicken your body!

The reason I could have faith in these words is not that I am a superwoman of faith. It is because I have seen the Lord work in others' lives, and because I believe His promises to us. Romans 10:17, *"So then faith cometh by hearing, and hearing by the word of God."* Get a scripture CD like I made or make your own. Listen to it over and over again to build yourself up in God's Words of healing.

I was able to have surgery and go to choir the night of the surgery with no pain or pain pills. The next day, I was on my way to Bible Study, and my garage door opener quit. I had to raise it manually for a couple of days even though I was not supposed to lift things. Oops, now my doctor knows I did that! I don't suggest you do what I did! Use wisdom!!!!!!

On my way to a prayer meeting the next night, I got my finger caught in the fold of the garage door but didn't lose the nail or have a bruised finger. I sang in the choir five days after the surgery, but realized that was pushing it. As we swayed from side to side, there was a slight pull on the stitches. The Holy Ghost showed me to hold on to my robe to relieve the pull. **It is persevering with the Word that causes you to win!** I choose to fight life through with the Word because I know it is true. You can, too!

Someone I thought was a faithful friend, called with a verbal attack seven days after surgery. Forty-eight hours before, she had offered to help with whatever I needed. Even though I had kept going and had great victory, my body was still in a fight with the spirit of death. But the devil does not play fair, and he had to try one last thing to take me out.

Fortunately, I recognized the devil's tactics, but it still hurt me deeply. The Holy Spirit had tried to warn me about the person, but I tried to believe the best. I called a few friends to have them pray, but did not say a lot to too many people. I recognized the devil's tactics because he tried a similar thing back in 1994 after my second surgery.

I had to stand and believe that chemo would not be the doctor's final plan for the follow-up to surgery. I really had to take my thoughts captive (2 Cor 10:4-5).

As a school teacher, I always planned way in advance. I had to keep myself from planning who would help me go to chemo treatments. Every time the urge to plan would come up, I refused to plan for what I did not expect to take place. With the help of the Father, Jesus, and Holy Spirit, I was able to cast down those thoughts.

The doctor did not even mention chemo again. Thank you, Jesus! The doctor had me take a pill called Arimidex. I did have to start back on a schedule of visits every three months instead of once a year.

Chapter 5

Adventure of 2005

The word for 2005 was to be alive and thrive and be revived! That was truly true for me! In January, along with all my regular activities, I attended one of the Charles and Frances Hunter's Advanced Healing Schools. In February, I went with the Adult Fellowship to Dallas for fun and shopping and helping with Pastor Joel Osteen's Dallas Event. The year got off to a great start! Life was full as usual!

Upon returning from Dallas, I started another adventure which had the potential to challenge my being alive, thriving, and being revived! When I went through my mail, I got my certificate from the Hunters for completing the Advanced Healing School. I also received a notice that my mammogram had a spot and I needed more testing. It was interesting that those two things came in the same batch of mail.

I went for further testing and then to the surgeon in mid-March. We scheduled surgery for April 4. I wanted it to be after Easter this time. We had our Easter service at Minute Maid Park again, and I wanted to be there. It was great!

On Monday, April 4, I had a mastectomy because I did not want to go this route again. Since my lymph nodes had been taken in 1994, it was day surgery. I was in at 6 AM and out by 1:30 PM.

Once again, I was blessed that the anesthesia put me out immediately. Once surgery was over and I was out of recovery, I was ready to go. I made it a fun time making screeching tire sounds as they wheeled me into the OR, and beeping sounds that moved people out of the way as they took me out to the car in a wheelchair at discharge. The wheel chair was used only because it is hospital regulations. My discharge nurse remembered me from last year. Most people are solemn with operations, but I chose to have a fun time in the midst of the event. Psalm 118:14 says: "*The Lord is my strength and song, and is become my salvation.*"

This time I did have a challenge that I had not had before. The enemy told me that I would die on the operating table or be impaired from the anesthesia and have pain. I kept that to myself except for telling two friends before surgery. Well, none of those things happened! I have never had pain or pain pills after an operation because of Isaiah 53:4. I hung onto the Word and the fact that in 2005, I would be alive and thrive and be revived.

I was originally told not to drive for a week. Of course, I would not let that keep me from the meetings and activities I had. I had precious friends that drove me to them. I had a drain in me from the surgery, but I camouflaged it and went on. When the drain came out that Thursday, I asked if I could drive. I got an early go-ahead, but I only drove close to home until the original week was up.

As it turned out, they only found a microscopic cell of cancer. It had mostly been scar tissue. For some reason, I had to wait three to four weeks for the final report, and to find out what treatment would be suggested. That was a long time! I kept saying no chemo and no radiation! Well, no chemo and no radiation and continuing on Arimidex with three month check-ups and blood work were the final verdict. Thank you, Jesus!

Just because I got back in the swing of things, I did take time to rest. Your body needs time to repair. In October of 2005, I had a burst of energy that I had not had. The Holy Spirit said that was restoration from 2004. It was not until the summer of 2006 that I got that burst of energy from the 2005 surgery.

Chapter 6

How can this happen?

hy did someone who believes in and proclaims healing and has healing scriptures in her get cancer? I even took a stand against cancer in my life years before it attacked me. Why? First of all, we have an enemy who has come to steal, kill, and destroy (John 10:10). He hates me and he hates you! Besides that, I overdo at times which affects my immune system.

Some of the other major attacks and miracles of my life:

- At 6 months old, I fell out of my crib;

- My salvation at about 5 years old;

- At age 5-6 I was pulled out of a pool before I was about to drown;

- At age 13, at my mother's funeral, the Father spoke to me and told me not to worry, she was in Heaven with Him and the Lord Jesus and the Holy Spirit who kept worldly grief from me;

- ✿ At age 16, I walked away from a car wreck (where the car flipped over 3 times and was totaled) and just went on to school;

- ✿ For 11 years, the Holy Spirit battled the hopelessness in my life and kept me from thoughts of suicide (I John 4:4);

- ✿ I have been through 4 cancer operations and I am alive and well;

- ✿ Jesus has provided me with a good job, bought me a house, given me ministry opportunities, good friends, and I could go on and on.

Oh, I started to fall from the top of a flight of stairs and broke my little finger, but caught my balance half way down, thanks to my angels. I questioned the Father about this since I had never broken a bone before. He said, *"the fall was meant to break your neck."* When I heard those words, I was happy with just a broken finger. The devil was the one that wanted me to have a broken neck, but the Father sent His angels to stop the evil plan.

The Lord told me before my first surgery that "I win in every situation." **No matter what comes our way, we win! Not because of who we are, but Whose we are**. We win because Jesus won for us! We are victors, not survivors!

What He did for me, He will do for you! God is no respecter of persons (Acts 10:34)! **If you have not asked Jesus into your life, you can do so right now. Just ask!**

Pray: "Lord Jesus, I repent of my sins. Come into my heart and wash me clean. I confess that You are the only Son of Jehovah God the Father. I make You my Lord and Savior. Thank You for coming into my life today!"

Three things you need to learn from reading the Bible.

1. You need to know the Father, Jesus, and Holy Spirit.

2. You need to know about the enemy or the thief as he is called in John 10:10 (the devil).

3. You need to know who you are in Christ and our inheritance in Him.

John 14:6

Jesus saith unto him, "I am the way, the truth, and the life: no man cometh unto the Father, but by me."

Romans 10:9

"That if thou shalt confess with thy mouth the Lord Jesus, and shalt believe in thine heart that God hath raised him from the dead, thou shalt be saved."

Ephesians 2:8-9

"For by grace are ye saved through faith; and that not of yourselves: it is the gift of God: Not of works, lest any man should boast."

Let the joy of the Lord and the Truth of His Word dominate your circumstance! Remember, **cancer is not a death sentence. Cancer does not equal death** ($C \neq D$)! Cancer is a name, and it must bow to the name of

Jesus (Philippians 2:10). If God is for us, cancer cannot be against us (Romans 8:31)!

The Name of Jesus

cancer

(The name of Jesus is over cancer or any other infirmity!)

Remember, Jesus said, "I will never leave thee, nor forsake thee." Jesus is the same yesterday, today, and forever (Hebrews 13:5,8). **Call on Him and believe!** Be a prisoner of Hope (Zechariah 9:12)!

Here is a great confession.

Fill in the blank with your situation!

I am blessed and highly favored!

I am healed, delivered, set free, and live in victory and prosperity!

I'm still standing and I win because of the stripes of Jesus and His Blood!

_____ is under the name of Jesus.

The Lord is for me so _____ cannot be against me!

This light affliction of _____ is working a great and eternal weight of Glory!

During the first three battles, I took communion every day. The fourth time, I was not led to do that, but the night before surgery, I was at a church, and guess what? We had communion.

1 Corinthians 11:23-26

"23 For I have received of the Lord that which also I delivered unto you, that the Lord Jesus the same night in which he was betrayed took bread:

24 And when he had given thanks, he brake it, and said, 'Take, eat: this is my body, which is broken for you: this do in remembrance of me.'

25 After the same manner also he took the cup, when he had supped, saying, 'this cup is the new testament in my blood: this do ye, as oft as ye drink it, in remembrance of me.'

26 For as often as ye eat this bread, and drink this cup, ye do shew the Lord's death till he come.'"

I made declarations as I took communion. I took the bread (in my case a cracker) and broke it and declared in the heavenlies that **because of the stripes of Jesus, I was healed!** I took grape juice and declared that because Jesus shed **His Blood for me as The Final Sacrifice, I was in right standing with the Father.**

I led worship at a conference right after the second surgery and could not bring communion elements with me since I had no place in the hotel to keep them.

Jesus said to take the bread and wine as a symbol of the new covenant and to do it in His remembrance (Matthew 26:26-30). Well, I took symbolic bread and wine, broke my air bread, and drank air wine, and made my declarations. **Remember that God is looking at our heart and our motive first and foremost.**

Remember, cancer is a name and it must bow to the name of Jesus. Philippians 2:9-11 *"Wherefore God also hath highly exalted him, and **given him a name which is above every name:** 10) That at the name of Jesus every knee should bow, of things in heaven, and things in earth, and things under the earth; 11) And that every tongue should confess that Jesus Christ is Lord, to the glory of God the Father."*

Remember, you have a good report that trumps the report of cancer. I Peter 2:24 "Who his own self bare our sins in his own body on the tree, that we, being dead to sins, should live unto righteousness: **by whose stripes ye were healed**."

Do not fear telling people the report, so they can stand with you. Those that stand with you are stronger than anyone who lacks the faith to believe with you. You and the Lord are a majority regardless of who stands with you!

Chapter 7

The Tale of Three Ladies

*A*pparently, my mother was suspicious that something was going on in her, but fear kept her from going to the doctor. She went in November of 1962. She died of breast cancer in September 1963 because she waited too long.

Cancer is not a death sentence. If you suspect something, pray and get it checked out. Put your trust in God's promise of long life. Know that by the stripes of Jesus, you have been healed! Psalm 91:16 *"With long life will I satisfy him, and shew him my salvation."* Isaiah 53:5 (1 Peter 2:24) ... ***"and with His stripes we are healed."***

In 1981, I knew two ladies who were diagnosed with liver cancer. One taught the Bible, but had not been taught how to stand on the Word and fight with the Word. She looked at the diagnosis from the view of "if it is God's will." Unfortunately, she was dead within six months. She did not know **healing is God's will**. The other lady was sent home and given three weeks to live. The medical field had nothing to really offer her. She and her husband knew that healing was God's will. She got 40 scriptures that she took as her medicine daily, and still takes today. Her death sentence of only three weeks to live has turned into over 29 years and counting at the writing of this book. Because of the Word of God that she and her husband taught me, I am alive today!

Yes, the last lady I mentioned is Dodie Osteen. She knew the Word of God could triumph over cancer or anything else! **Get it settled in your heart, it is God's will that you live and declare His works!** Cancer does not have to be a death sentence. How are you looking at your situation? I hope it is that the Word works and is above everything!

One thing all three women had in common was that they had accepted Jesus as Lord and the only begotten Son of Jehovah God, the God of Abraham, Isaac, and Jacob. If you have not accepted Him as your Savior, ask Him into your heart today. Find a Bible-based church and get the Word of God in you!

Pray: "Lord Jesus, I repent of my sins. Come into my heart and wash me clean. I confess that You are the only Son of Jehovah, God the Father. I make You my Lord and Savior. Thank You for coming into my life today!"

I have the scriptures I stood on in the following chapters. I want to share them with you so that they will be life to you. This is the greatest treasure I can give you. I hope my testimony encourages you to stand on the Word. Jesus is Lord and His Name is above cancer or any other situation!

Chapter 8

Confessions of 1994

Scriptures I stood on:

Cancer cannot rise up a second time. (Nahum 1:9)

I am redeemed from the curse of the law! (Galatians 3:13)

By His stripes, I was healed (I Peter 2:24 and Isaiah 53:5)

I overcome by the Blood of the Lamb and the word of my testimony. (Revelation 12:11)

He has brought health and cure, and cured me and reveals unto me the abundance of peace and truth. (Jeremiah 33:6)

Because I have set my love upon Him, He will deliver me. With long life, He will satisfy me and show me His salvation. (Psalm 91:14)

He Is the Lord who healed me! (Exodus 15:26)

He forgives all my iniquities and heals all disease which attacks me. (Psalm 103:1)

...He will take sickness away from the midst of me ... the number of my days He will fulfill. (Exodus 23:25) (Deuteronomy 7:15)

He will restore health to me and heal me of my wounds. (Jeremiah 30:17)

Many are the afflictions of the righteous, BUT the Lord delivers us out of them all. (Psalm 34:19)

His word is in my heart like a burning fire shut up in my bones. (Jeremiah 20:9)

I give attention to His word. It does not depart my eyes. I keep it in the midst of my heart. It is life to me and health to all my flesh. (Proverbs 4:20-22)

I look unto Jesus the author and finisher of my faith. (Hebrews 12:2)

What is impossible with men is possible with my Father. (Matthew 19:26)

I wait for the Lord, My soul waits and in His word I do hope! (Psalm 130:5)

I will not fear for He is with me and holds my right hand ... those (cancer) who have increased against me, who strive against me and contend with me shall be as nothing. They shall perish! They shall be as nothing, as a nonexistent thing! (Isaiah 41:10-13)

That which my Father did not plant shall be uprooted! (Matthew 15:13)

Greater is He that is in me than he that is in the world! (1 John 4:4)

The same power that raised Jesus from the dead dwells in my mortal body and quickens (makes alive) my body! (Romans 8:11)

This light affliction Is but for a moment and is working a far more exceeding and eternal weight of glory! (2 Corinthians 4:17)

I shall lay hands on the sick and they shall recover! (Mark 16:18)

When they try to find the lump it shall be as nothing! Cancer cannot rise up a second time for I am redeemed! Out of the void He can create a new left breast! He did it for the earth and He can do it for me! (Genesis 1:2)

Also read:

Mark 11:23-24;

Psalm 23, 34, 37, 103,112,119, 121, 139;

Jeremiah 29:11;

Philippians 1:6, 2, 13

Chapter 9

Radiation Scriptures

Request for agreement in prayer:

1. No side effects or after effects!

2. No burned skin!

3. No change in my blood chemistry!

4. No change in my bones!

5. No adverse changes, only good!

6. All cancer cells to be destroyed forever!

Special Scripture Confessions for This Adventure;

I am blessed because I trust In the Lord who is my hope. I shall not fear when heat comes. My leaves will be green which means that my body will be as it was meant to be. (Jeremiah 17: 7-8)

When I am zapped with the radiation, I shall go through the fire, but I shall not be burned nor shall the flame scorch me. (Isaiah 43:2)

No weapon formed against me shall prosper and every tongue that rises against me shall be condemned for that is my heritage. (Isaiah 54:17)

The Lord is a shield about me. He is my glory and the lifter of my head! (Psalm 3:3)

The Lord is a sun and shield. He gives grace and glory. No good thing will He withhold from those who walk uprightly. I am blessed for I trust in Him. (Psalm 84:11-12)

The Lord is my strength and my song. He has become my salvation. (Psalm 118:14)

His Joy is my strength! (Nehemiah 8:10)

He will cleanse my blood and deliver me from blood guiltiness. (Joel 3:21)

I am redeemed and overcome by the Blood of the Lamb. I am locked in under the Blood. (Galatians 3:13 and Revelation 12:11)

I win in every situation! (Romans 8:37)

The thief has come to kill, steal, and destroy, but Jesus came that I might have life and life more abundantly. (John 10:10)

He will deliver me and satisfy me with long life. I will fulfill the plan the Father has for me. (Psalm 91:15-16)

He guards all my bones and none will be broken which means altered. (Psalm 34:20)

The radiation will do me good and no harm all the days of my life. (Proverbs 31:12)

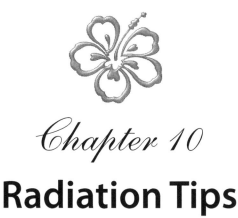

Chapter 10

Radiation Tips

Helpful Things During Radiation Treatments

(I did radiation in 1994, so some things may have changed.)

Things to buy beforehand :

Dark clothes or tops so marks will not ruin the clothes.

Cotton T shirts or tank tops - I like the tank tops because they are less bulky. These are worn under your clothes to protect clothes, and cotton breathes the best.

Cotton bras - leisure hook in the front are the best, I think.

Dark cotton night shirts for sleeping - again, because of markings.

Stool for tub/shower- I used a plastic square table usually for patios.

Shower head with hand held flexibility - I got an inexpensive one from a discount store and it lasted for years.

(The stool and shower head will allow you to take a shower and avoid the radiation area and rest. I had to wash my hair in the kitchen sink!)

First visit:

Wear something dark, so the marks will not ruin your clothes, if they rub off on it (cotton is best).

They will use a lot of equipment to determine the area to be radiated, fit blocks for that area, and mark the area with a pen. This area cannot have any water on it until after the treatments.

Depending on your skin-type, they will stay on or have to be re-marked each time.

During my five weeks of treatment:

The joy of the Lord is your strength!

You will go through the fire and not be burned nor shall the flame scorch you!

Much rest!!!

Reduce all activities!!!!!!!!!!!!!!!!!!!!!!!!!!!!!!!!

I laid hands on all the gowns in the dressing areas.

I didn't read about the effects of radiation or what they say to do until after the treatments. I did not want that in my head. I only wanted my confession.

A friend tried to tell me that radiation reduced his energy level. I knew mine would not be diminished, but I learned that my flesh was not as strong as my spirit. The body takes time to heal!

If at all possible, let someone drive you!

Take it easy! Don't push!

I pushed too much!!!! *It was not wise!* The Father was soooooo *merciful* to me!!!

Resting and regaining your strength are the most important things! Everything else will survive!

Take naps or sleep late! Your body needs the rest!

Chapter 11

Scriptures of 2004

Isaiah 53:1; 4-5

"1 Who has believed our report? And to whom has the arm of the Lord been revealed?

4 Surely He has borne our griefs And carried our sorrows; Yet we esteemed Him stricken, smitten by God, and afflicted.

5 But He was wounded for our transgressions, He was bruised for our iniquities; The chastisement for our peace was upon Him, And by His stripes we are healed."

Romans 8:11, 31

"11 But if the Spirit of Him who raised Jesus from the dead dwells in you, He who raised Christ from the dead will also give life to your mortal bodies through His Spirit Who dwells in you.

31 What then shall we say to these things? If God is for us, who can be against us?"

Matthew 15:13

"But He answered and said, 'Every plant which My heavenly Father has not planted will be uprooted.'"

44

Isaiah 54:17

"No weapon formed against you shall prosper, And every tongue which rises against you in judgment You shall condemn. This is the heritage of the servants of the Lord, And their righteousness is from Me," says the Lord."

Psalm 119: 49-50

"49 Remember the word to Your servant, Upon which You have caused me
to hope.
50 This is my comfort in my affliction, For Your word has given me life."

Jeremiah 30:17

"For I will restore health to you And I will heal you of thy wounds,' says the Lord,..."

Jeremiah 17:14

"Heal me, O Lord, and I shall be healed; Save me, and I shall be saved, For You are my praise."

Psalm 91:1-2

"1 He who dwells in the secret place of the Most High Shall abide under the shadow of the Almighty.
2 I will say of the Lord, 'He is my refuge and my fortress; my God, in Him I will trust'. "

Chapter 12

Scriptures of 2005

1 Corinthians 16:9

"For a great and effective door has opened to me, and there are many adversaries."

2 Corinthians 4:17

"For our light affliction, which is but for a moment, is working for us a far more exceeding and eternal weight of glory."

Habakkuk 3:17-19

"17 Though the fig tree may not blossom, Nor fruit be on the vines; Though the labor of the olive may fail, And the fields yield no food; Though the flock may be cut off from the fold, And there be no herd in the stalls--

18 Yet I will rejoice in the Lord, I will joy in the God of my salvation (I will praise Thee, oh God!).

19 The Lord God is my strength; He will make my feet like deer's feet, And He will make me walk on my high hills."

You can begin today to have that same

"7 Return to your rest, O my soul, For the Lord has dealt bountifully with you.

For You have delivered my soul from death, My eyes from tears, And my feet from falling.

9 I will walk before the Lord in the land of the living."

Psalm 118:14-17

"14 The Lord is my strength and song, And He has become my salvation.

The voice of rejoicing and salvation is in the tents of the righteous; The right hand of the Lord does valiantly.

16 The right hand of the Lord is exalted; The right hand of the Lord does valiantly.

17 I shall not die, but live, And declare the works of the Lord."

Isaiah 53:4-5

"4 Surely He has borne our griefs and carried our sorrows (pain); Yet we esteemed Him stricken, Smitten by God, and afflicted.

5 But He was wounded for our transgressions, He was bruised for our iniquities; The chastisement for our peace was upon Him, and by His stripes we are healed."

1 Peter 2:24

"Who Himself bore our sins in His own body on the tree, that we, having died to sins, might live for righteousness: by whose stripes you were healed."

Galatians 3:13

"Christ has redeemed us from the curse of the law, being made a curse for us: for it is written, 'Cursed is everyone who hangeth on a tree.'"

Matthew 15:13

"But He answered and said, 'Every plant which My heavenly Father has not planted will be uprooted.' "

Revelation 12:11

"And they overcame him by the blood of the Lamb and by the word of their testimony, and they did not love their lives unto the death."

Romans 8:11

"But if the Spirit of Him who raised Jesus from the dead dwells in you, He who raised Christ from the dead will also give life to your mortal bodies through His Spirit who dwells in you."15

Romans 8:31-32

"31 What then shall we say to these things? If God is for us, who can be against us?

32 He who did not spare His own Son, but delivered Him up for us all, how shall He not with Him also freely give us all things?"

Romans 8:37-39

"37 Yet in all these things we are more than conquerors through Him who loved us.

38 For I am persuaded that neither death nor life, nor angels nor principalities nor powers, nor things present nor things to come,

39 nor height nor depth, nor any other created thing, shall be able to separate us from the love of God which is in Christ Jesus our Lord."

Ephesians 6: 12-13

"12 For we do not wrestle against flesh and blood, but against principalities, against powers, against the rulers of the darkness of this age, against spiritual hosts of wickedness in the heavenly places.

13 Therefore take up the whole armor of God, that you may be able to withstand in the evil day, and having done all, to stand."

2 Thessalonians 3:3

"But the Lord is faithful, who will establish you and guard you from the evil one."

I am blessed and highly favored!

I am healed, delivered, set free, and live in victory!

I'm still standing and I win because of the Stripes of Jesus and His Blood!

_____ is under the name of Jesus.

The Lord is for me so _____ cannot be against me!

This light affliction of _____ is working a great and eternal weight of Glory!

Chapter 13

2011

(P.S. The Devil is a Liar)

ell, I was about to do the last read-through of the first 12 chapters and decided I need to add this chapter after my latest experience. It was a battle of the mind over a bone scan, situations, and words.

In mid-September, I began to have a pain in the right side of my chest. I tried stretching, but no relief! I was concerned since it did not go away. When I went in for my yearly check-up with my cancer surgeon, he became concerned. He scheduled a nuclear bone scan, and said, "it (breast cancer) likes to hide in the bones." I would not receive nor repeat those words!

Right after that appointment, I went for my 6 month check-up with my oncologist. She did routine blood tests. Two of them are CA tests, which are tumor makers. The results of that came back, and all was fine with the blood. That was a positive thought to fight with!

I go to a massage therapist and chiropractor once a month. When I went to the massage therapist, I told her about the pain. She worked on the pectoral or fan muscle from the back. Usually, it is a muscle that a swimmer would have problems with. After the massage, the Holy Spirit showed me what I had been doing to strain the muscle. I had been given a new Apple Laptop and classes to learn more about the computer. I would sit in the driver's seat and, with my right arm, would lift the computer up and into the back seat, straining the fan muscle. Another good positive thought as to what was going on!

Prior to this a friend had told me to take care of myself. I had so many situations, where I was helping friends. I do try to rest because of my past experiences with running my immune system down. Of course, I don't always do it!

If you will remember, adventure number three in Chapter 4 occurred after I neglected to heed a warning in 2004 to slow down and take care of myself. Naturally, the enemy started using that against my mind in this situation. "See, that was a warning; cancer is in your bones!" Of course too, my bones ached some, and that added to the negative thoughts in my mind. Also, my chest pain was not totally gone.

For about a week and a half, the negative thoughts were trying to win. A friend prayed for me and they stopped until the day I was having the test done. I ended up waiting for 25 minutes because no one told them I was waiting. The enemy started in with a vengeance as I waited.

I had been told I would be in a gown for 2 hours for the nuclear die to do its thing and could not use a computer. Okay, that was not true. I was to stay in my clothes and wait in the lobby. They suggested I eat something while I was waiting. So, I could have worked on the computer but I didn't have it. My emotions broke, and the tears started. When that happened, it was hard to stop, particularly since I was tired that day.

With tears still coming down, I went to get a bite to eat. I finally got a little less teary-eyed and went back to the lobby to wait. I listened to a few sweet messages on my phone from friends. I didn't want to return them then because it would start the tears all over again. Tears are an emotional release and are a blessing from the Lord. However, in this instance, I didn't want people staring. And, please, don't let the tears ruin the eye make-up!

The chapel was right by where I was waiting. I decided to go in and sing to the Lord! I had to stop twice when someone else came in, but started up again when I was the only human in the place. After 15-20 minutes, I decided I had better go back so they could find me. I had barely sat down when they came to get me.

I was suppose to lie on the table as a donut-shaped camera scanned my body. It takes about an hour. I think I fell asleep a few times. The tech said I did a great job since you are suppose to not move during the scan. She asked me a question; "So because of pain, your doctor ordered the test?" As she asked, I saw the images and was not sure what was lit up on them! Those were two more things the enemy used against my mind.

In 2007, the orthopedist sent me for an MRI of my knee. The tech asked me why he sent me. I said I have a cyst behind my knee. They responded "oh, yes!" That brought a little concern as to what they saw, but we got the results of that back right away. They had been shocked at the size of the cyst, as was the doctor. It was a ten cubic inch cyst. That is 2" X 5" X 1"! Huge! That is a whole other God story. We fixed the torn meniscus that was causing it. The Lord had awakened me up at 3AM and told me to go to the doctor in that case. Imagine if that had burst! I might have lost my leg!

So, the words the tech spoke after the bone scan made me think there was a problem. Seeing a glowing image on the scan and those words resonated in my mind because of my prior experience. The fight to not accept those words and image was on.

The night of the scan, the Lakewood Choir, of which I am a member, was asked to sing at TD Jakes' meeting. Paula White spoke on "You have a story" and "Sing O Barren ... break forth into singing ... " from Isaiah 54:1. I thought, I just lived that this afternoon!

Do I have a story to tell! You have read about this part of my story, but I could write many more books. Recently, I had to read a book about trauma for a certain organization. I did not like the book because it was more on man helping you through tragedy and not the Holy

Spirit. The one thing I got out of it was how my life has been filled with tragedy. There were only maybe two I had not gone through! Thank you, Holy Spirit, for bringing me through!

Well, for about a week after the scan it was a mental fight to fight negative thoughts. I chose to cast them down, but they didn't stop until a week before I actually got the results. Going home from Bible study, I realized if I had a report of bone cancer, the enemy would not have been fighting me so hard. I called the devil a liar! A friend called that afternoon talking about what God had showed her about a situation, and it confirmed what I had decided. From that moment until the day I got the report, those voices were quiet. They did try the night before I got the results but Ha! Ha!, I win because of Jesus, The Word!

The report came back twelve days after the scan. No trace of cancer! The devil is a liar! No chemo or any other treatment!

I decided to also add scriptures about bones in Chapter 14. I got these out and used them in this battle of the mind! In the late eighties, I wanted to find bone scriptures for a lady going through bone cancer. Some of these are repeat scriptures from the others in the book, but that is okay!

Before all this latest adventure started, I redid the tape I made of healing scriptures into a CD. I started playing it every night to put me to sleep and minister to my spirit man! Jesus is Lord and the devil is a liar!

Chapter 14

Bone Scriptures

I have found several scriptures on bones. Many seem to talk about broken bones which is good but I had wanted to find some for people to stand when their bones had been attacked by some other infirmity. I decided to look up the word "broken" and found some good news.

Broken:

❀ Damaged or altered by or as if by breaking (They don't have to be actually broken but just altered!)

❀ Violated by transgression (Violated by abnormal cells)

❀ Disrupted by change (Changed by abnormal cells)

❀ Of a flower (We are special flowers to the Lord.) having an irregular, streaked or blotched pattern especially from from virus infection.

- ❀ Made weak or infirm
- ❀ Subdued; crushed
- ❀ Cut off: disconnected
- ❀ Not complete or full

Psalm 34:19-20

"Many are the afflictions of the righteous but the LORD delivers him out of them all. He guards all his bones not one of them is broken."

Proverbs 3:7-8

"Do not be wise in your own eyes. Fear the LORD and depart from evil. It will be health to your flesh and strength to your bones."

Proverbs 15:30

"The light of the eyes rejoices the heart and a good report makes the bones healthy."

(We have a good report I Peter 2:24!)

1 Peter 2:24

" ... by whose stripes you are healed."

(Our good report!)

Proverbs 16:24

"Pleasant words are like a honeycomb. Sweetness to the soul and health to the bones."

Nehemiah 8:10

" ... this day is holy to our Lord. Do not Sorrow, for the Joy of the LORD is your strength."

Isaiah 53:4

"Surely He has borne our griefs and sorrows ..."

Proverbs 17:22

"A merry heart does good like medicine but a broken spirit dries the bones"

Ezekiel 37:4,11-14

"... Prophesy to these bones, and say to them. 'O dry bones hear the word of the Lord!' ... 'I will put My Spirit in you, and you shall live, and I will place you in your own land. Then you will know that I the LORD, have spoken it and performed it,' says the Lord."

Jeremiah 20:9

" ... But His word was In my heart like a burning fire shut up In my bones ..."

It is important to find scriptures about your particular situation. It Is important to stand on them by getting them into your heart and your mouth. Proverbs 4:20-22 says, "My son, give attention to my word; incline your ear to my sayings. Do not let them depart from your eyes; keep them in the midst of your heart; for they are life to those who find them and health to all their flesh."

The Word must be mixed with faith. "The word which they heard did not profit them, not being mixed with faith." (Hebrews 4:2) "Faith is the substance of things hoped for, the evidence of things not seen." (Hebrews 11:1) "Look unto Jesus, the author and finisher of our faith." (Hebrews 12:2) Jesus had to have faith that the Father would raise Him from the dead!

"Keep your heart with all diligence for out of it spring the issues of life." (Proverbs 4:23) Broken-hearted means crushed by grief and sorrow. Don't let grief and sorrow crush you. Isaiah 53:4 says that, " He has borne our griefs and carried our sorrows." "With men this is impossible, but with God all things are possible." (Matthew 19:26) In Psalm 130:5, David said, "I wait for the Lord, my soul waits and in His Word I do hope!"

Isaiah 66:14

"...your heart shall rejoice and your bones shall flourish like grass ... "

Isaiah 41:10-13

"Fear not, for I am with you; Be not dismayed, for I am your God. I will strengthen you, Yes, I will help you, I will uphold you with My righteous right hand. Behold, all those who were incensed against you shall be ashamed and disgraced; They shall be as nothing, and those who strive with you shall perish. You shall seek them and not find them— Those who contended with you. Those who war against you shall be as nothing, as a nonexistent thing. 'For I, the LORD your God, will hold your right hand, Saying to you, Fear not, I will help you.' "

Hebrews 13:5

"... For He Himself has said, 'I will never leave you nor forsake you!' "

Battles are not always easy or won overnight, but we do overcome and we do win! Revelation 12:11 says, "They overcame by the blood of the Lamb and by the word of their testimony." 1 John 4:4 says, " ... He who is in you is greater than he who is in the world." Romans 8:37 says, "Yet in all these things we are more than conquerors through Him that loved us."

Quote this paraphrase of Hebrews 11:11! "___(your name)___, herself (himself) received strength to fight the devil and__(cancer,etc.)__. She (He) overcame by the blood of the Lamb and the word of her(his) testimony (Revelations 12:11). She(He) was victorious because she(he) judged Him faithful who had promised!"

"Now thanks be to God who always leads us in triumph ..." (2 Corinthians 2:14)

We win in every situation!

"For your light affliction, which is but for a moment, is working for us a far more exceeding and eternal weight of Glory!" (2 Corinthians 4:17))

Epilogue

Jesus has done this for me, and He will do it for you! The Word works for a cold or cancer or any situation! God has good plans for you no matter what your situation looks like. Jeremiah 29:11 says "For I know the thoughts that I think toward you, saith the LORD, thoughts of peace, and not of evil, to give you a future and a hope."

God is a loving Father. I hope you know Him as a Father and not just a distant God. If you don't, ask Him to reveal Himself to you as a Father. 1 John 4:8 ... *"God is love."*

Do you need peace? Ask Jesus for His peace! He said, *"Peace I leave with you, My peace I give unto you; not as the world gives, give do I to you. Let not your heart be troubled, neither let it be afraid."* (John 14:27)

Do you need comfort? John 14:16 *"And I will pray the Father, and He shall give you another Helper, that He may abide with you forever."* John 14:26 *"But the **Helper, which is the Holy Ghost**, whom the Father will send in My name, He will teach you all things, and bring all things to your remembrance, whatsoever I have said unto you."* John 15:26 *"But when the Comforter is come, whom I will send* *unto you from the Father, even the Spirit of truth, which proceedeth from the Father, He shall testify of me."*

Peace and joy will take you a lot farther than fear in any situation! With man, things are often impossible; but with God they are not impossible (Matthew 19:26, Mark 10:27, Luke 18:27).

I hope this book has encouraged you! May the peace of God abide in you forever!

Linda

Made in the USA
Lexington, KY
31 July 2013